BOLD
Self-Reflection

Know Thyself

TERRI M. BOLDS
MS, LPC

Copyright © 2019 by Terri M. Bolds
All rights reserved.
Printed and Bound in the United States

Published by
Bold Visions Consulting
(513) 299-8177
www.boldvisionsconsulting.com

Cover and Interior Design: TWA Solutions.com

ISBN: 978-1-7330563-9-7

All rights reserved. No part of this book may be reproduced, stored in a retrieval system or transmitted in any form or by any means without the prior written permission of the publisher—except by a reviewer who may quote brief passages in a review to be printed in a newspaper, magazine or journal.

This book is not intended as a substitute for the medical advice of physicians or licensed mental health professionals. The reader should regularly consult a physician or mental health professional in matters relating to his/her health/mental health and particularly with respect to any symptoms that may require diagnosis or medical attention.

For inquiries, speaking engagements, book signings, literary events, contact: boldcounselor3@gmail.com.

Dedicated to my late cousin, Kevin, who photographed me often. I want to use those photos to tell a story.

Table of Contents

Introduction 7

Own It..9

Greatness is You 16

Wonder Why..20

Relationships 21

Friendships 29

I Smile 36

Let *It* Go 38

Self-You 44

Gratitude 47

Introduction

Many times, people walk around, living their lives, not knowing why or how they ended up the way they are. Have you ever met someone whose complaining is endless, whose unhappiness for others is never ending, who's in constant failed relationships, or just can't seem to get it right? There is a reason behind that person's behaviors and attitudes. When we see a person, we see the physical shell, but don't consider that we are also meeting their past, hurts, trauma, ups, downs, joys, and pains. As a therapist, I look beyond the shell. My focus is from a cognitive-behavioral approach. I want people to understand how their thoughts, feelings, behaviors, and outcomes are all connected.

Travel this journey as we explore how so many people struggle with some areas of life. I have used photographs of myself taken by my late cousin. He used to tell me he loved photographing me and how amazing I was. Building up self-worth is a hard task, but the people in my life refuse to let me think less of myself, which makes me grateful. The following pages will encourage self-exploration and great change.

Own It

Let's start with HONESTY!

Now, this section may seem a little harsh to some, but it is necessary to introduce conflict, to get to the root cause of things. Ladies, at some point, deflection has to be a non-factor in your life in order for maturation. Social media is a platform for a person to be anyone they desire to be—a "cool kid" as an adult, with the subconscious hope of winning the most popular superlative never received in years passed. Having all the fame you did not acquire in your youth. The filters and "likes"

elevate your self-worth to a point of delusion. While living your best delusional life, you suppress the truth like a broken record.

Don't forget the YOU in the situations that stand out in your mind, as the result of and contributions of others that led to unfavorable outcomes. When you say things like, "Men ain't nothing," or "I can't trust anyone," or "Who needs friends?" or "Keep me out of your drama," without owning the roles you play in these now befitting biblical commandments, "thy shall not like your baby daddy," and "thou shall think everyone is shady," and "thou shall be heartless and lonely," and "thou shall be messy," the YOU gets more diluted to the point of saturation.

It is important that you own the YOU in situations. Everyone is not out to get you, some things are your fault, and you contribute to both favorable and unfavorable situations. Once you realize that YOU have some responsibility just as THEY, maturation can begin. No, you may not cause all your child's father using you, but YOU are picking them. No you may not be the gossip of the group, but YOU keep coming up in every conflict. Owning the YOU in situations removes the victim role that you were oblivious to creating with delusional thinking.

Let's address the YOU. When you think of any situation in your life where turning the cheek at the reflection in the mirror is a constant, answer these questions:

1. What part of the situation can I honestly own?
2. Was there a way I could have changed the outcome?
3. What red signs did I ignore?
4. What state of mind was I in at the time?
5. What seems to be my pattern of behavior?

Now that we addressed the role we play in the conflict of our lives, let's address another big elephant in the room. Lack of self-love. Some confuse pampering yourself, or taking trips as self-love. The self-love I am talking about is loving the person you are when you go to bed at night and wake up in the morning, loving yourself when you look in the mirror, loving yourself when someone else is living the life you want, loving yourself past your flaws, mistakes, and hurts. I am talking about believing in your worth, believing you matter, believing your life has purpose, believing you didn't deserve to be mistreated, abused, or thrown away. Sometimes, our lack of self-love causes us to bask in negative situations, like those mentioned above. Those behaviors are a mask to cover up the real you. Bringing hell to places around you because heaven seems beyond your reach.

    Take this exercise and do a self-love check. First, write all the things about yourself that you view as negative, unappealing, hurtful and/or damaging about yourself in the space provided beside the broken mirror. In the space provided beside the unbroken mirror, write all the positive things you feel about yourself or the things you would like to feel about yourself when you look in the mirror.

Cracked Mirror Questions

_____
_____
_____
_____
_____

1. Why do those things stick out to you?

_____
_____
_____
_____
_____
_____

2. Do you know when these feelings started?

_____
_____

3. Is this something you will put in the work to change?

Complete Mirror Questions

_____
_____
_____
_____
_____

1. Are these things you believe about yourself or hope to someday?

_____
_____
_____
_____
_____
_____

2. If they are things you hope to believe, what things can you do to get to that point?

_____
_____

3. How will you maintain the positive beliefs you have about yourself?

Greatness Is You
by Terri M. Bolds

I see you gazing in the distance searching

For purpose and security

Longing for the split second that you realize your existence was intended

Hoping for the fairy book love story you've read about since your youth

The career that big mama brags to all the church mothers about

For the crowd to stop at your entry.

Have you ever really looked at you?

You the one that has overcome trial after trial

That has stared life in the face and dared it to try you

Who overcame that person that tried to break you down

That breathed life into that thing you never you thought you could

So stop gazing, waiting for the descension of an imaginable you

God already sent you; Greatness IS YOU.

Sunday	Monday	Tuesday	We...

BOLD SELF-LOVE NOTES

	WRITE A POSITVE PHRASE TO YOURSELF EACH DAY		
Thursday		Friday	Saturday

Wonder Why
By Terri M. Bolds

No wonder why you feel this way
It seems that you regret each day
That you're here,
for fear of what's near
It's always unclear and you look like a deer
In headlights wondering when the smoke will clear
Wondering when that straggling tear will die
Constantly wondering why and ending each night with a sigh
No wonder why you feel this way
But you do know today can be a new way
To view the path that appeared so drab
Now there's hope you can grab
To sprinkle on the thoughts that leave you mad
You have the power to change your way
And let every day be a new be a new day.

Relationships

The Creator created romantic relationships. It is natural for living things to have the desire for sex, intimacy, and affection from a romantic partner. As imperfect beings, the quest to fulfill the need can sometimes turn into a disaster. We take control of our situations and try to ignore the signs and, many times, the little voices in our heads that some may refer to as the Holy Spirit, or our conscience. I am a perfect example of that very thing.

At thirty-two years old, I decided I was ready to date. I, along with some friends and family, joined a few dating sites and played around. Well, one particular guy was active in his pursuit. It led to a date. I can still recall worrying about my outfit and hair. My cousin helped me get dressed and did my makeup; I was all set. He changed the location and time. He got there and he was "smacked," which means very unattractive to me. He said he was thirty-four, but I kept thinking, *He is an old looking thirty-four-year-old man.* As time went on, we became exclusive. I was in constant turmoil and confusion with him. All things I believed were happening he was somehow twisting and telling me things I knew made no sense. For example, I only talked to him when he was in the car. We had a date scheduled, so he could meet my mother. He made up some excuse why he could not meet us, while my mother and I were at the restaurant, waiting on him. There were several signs of him cheating, but the last time was different. This time, someone whom I love like a sister presented information to me that was undeniable. I addressed him and he lied. At that point, it was over and it devastated me.

Fast forward a week later and I was talking to a friend about the situation, who asked for his information. I don't know about you, but I have family and friends who are worse than the FBI. They will find any information on a person you'll ever need. We attempted to look him up early on, but couldn't find anything because I had the wrong spelling of his name. So not only was he seven years older than what he said, he was also a very married man. I was dating a married man, who was also dating other women. At that point, we had all of his information, including address. My squad was ready to pull up to his house, but I just couldn't let that happen. Oh, but his cheating ways caught up with him and Karma came back around for me to see.

So now I was left to my thoughts. I was with someone else's husband. I wondered how God would ever forgive me. I felt so dirty. That night in the shower, I scrubbed myself so hard. I threw away anything that resembled him. For at least a month, I panicked each time I saw a car that resembled his. It terrified me. This man had scarred my life forever, and I could have prevented it all.

That back story was to bring me to this point; I didn't trust myself. When I rehash that experience, I recall the back and forth conversations I had with people, doubting myself when my gut, the Holy Spirit, and my conscience told me at first sight that I was entertaining a fraud. My previous experiences created a strong distrust for people. So, I challenged myself not to let that crutch paralyze me any longer. What I didn't understand was that trusting and being smart were two different entities. Stevie Wonder could see that the situation I was in was hazardous. My grandmother used to tell me she had a bad feeling about things and one day, she had a dream and told me her dreams were not wrong. She was right, although I never told her in detail; she knew.

Why did I let myself endure such pain, confusion and stress? I was not paying attention to my CBT Model. Cognitive Behavioral Therapy demonstrates how our thoughts and feelings affect our behaviors. In my book, *Bold Love: A Letter to My Young Sisters*, I created a visual model I was still learning myself.

Triggers (events) ➡ Thoughts (feelings) ➡ Behavior ➡ Outcome

I needed a visual. With the model, I can insert various situations in the flow to assist with my outcomes, but to also help to increase awareness of how situations affect my behavior. I let myself be "played," as they say, because I didn't understand my CBT flow. At the time, I didn't know how to differentiate between trust and truth. Truth was that my trust was being misused. Truth was, the red flags were endless and I continued to ignore the truth to increase my trust. Truth is, there is a lesson in every situation. That situation led me back to therapy. I was depressed, I cut my hair and I gained weight that is still present with me to this day, plus more.

Reality is, we all "play the fool," at some point. And for some of us, studies show that negative and hard experiences are inevitable for many of us. The more trauma, abuse and neglect we experience as a child sets us up for higher health risks and negative outcomes.

"An ACE score is a tally of different types of abuse, neglect, and other hallmarks of a rough childhood. According to the Adverse Childhood Experiences study, the rougher your childhood, the higher your score is likely to be and the higher your risk for later health problems"(https://www.npr.org/sections/health-shots/2015/03/02/387007941/take-the-ace-quiz-and-learn-what-it-does-and-doesnt-mean) ."You get one point for each type of trauma. The higher your ACE score, the higher your risk of health and social problems. ... As your ACE score increases, so does the risk of disease, social and emotional problems. With an ACE score of 4 or more, things start getting serious"(https://acestoohigh.com/got-your-ace-score/).

Take the ACE test view your results.

Statistics exist, but so does God who surpasses all things. Having a hard childhood is not a death sentence. It is important that we be honest with ourselves and to learn ourselves. We have the power to change our outcomes. You don't have to be in an abusive relationship. You don't have to stand victim to emotional trauma. You don't have to accept mediocrity. Understand that you are worthy. You are worthy enough for you. Be worthy enough to yourself, to not subject yourself to emotional or physical abuse. More women than you know have endured some hard situations that they don't discuss, done things they would never reveal or live in situations that cause mental torment. Our desire to have intimacy, sex, romance and companionship creates this idea of "I'll take what I can get." WRONG! You want what God has prepared for you. You want someone that won't have you questioning your

Bold Self-Reflection: Know Thyself | 25

Adverse Childhood Experience (ACE) Questionnaire
Finding your ACE Score ra hbr 10 24 06

While you were growing up, during your first 18 years of life:

1. Did a parent or other adult in the household **often** …
    Swear at you, insult you, put you down, or humiliate you?
    or
    Act in a way that made you afraid that you might be physically hurt?
    Yes   No   If yes enter 1   _____

2. Did a parent or other adult in the household **often** …
    Push, grab, slap, or throw something at you?
    or
    Ever hit you so hard that you had marks or were injured?
    Yes   No   If yes enter 1   _____

3. Did an adult or person at least 5 years older than you **ever**…
    Touch or fondle you or have you touch their body in a sexual way?
    or
    Try to or actually have oral, anal, or vaginal sex with you?
    Yes   No   If yes enter 1   _____

4. Did you **often** feel that …
    No one in your family loved you or thought you were important or special?
    or
    Your family didn't look out for each other, feel close to each other, or support each other?
    Yes   No   If yes enter 1   _____

5. Did you **often** feel that …
    You didn't have enough to eat, had to wear dirty clothes, and had no one to protect you?
    or
    Your parents were too drunk or high to take care of you or take you to the doctor if you needed it?
    Yes   No   If yes enter 1   _____

6. Were your parents **ever** separated or divorced?
    Yes   No   If yes enter 1   _____

7. Was your mother or stepmother:
    Often pushed, grabbed, slapped, or had something thrown at her?
    or
    Sometimes or often kicked, bitten, hit with a fist, or hit with something hard?
    or
    Ever repeatedly hit over at least a few minutes or threatened with a gun or knife?
    Yes   No   If yes enter 1   _____

8. Did you live with anyone who was a problem drinker or alcoholic or who used street drugs?
    Yes   No   If yes enter 1   _____

9. Was a household member depressed or mentally ill or did a household member attempt suicide?
    Yes   No   If yes enter 1   _____

10. Did a household member go to prison?
    Yes   No   If yes enter 1   _____

Now add up your "Yes" answers: _____ **This is your ACE Score**

appearance. You want someone who wants you. You want someone who believes in you. You want someone who prays for you. You want someone who loves you. You want someone who wants to be with you in public and behind closed doors. You want someone who encourages you. You want someone who understands you. You want someone who gives you butterflies. Accepting "what you can get" is not any of that.

The age-old question, "Why do people cheat?", in my opinion, it is because everyone is searching to fulfill their needs. We all have needs we are seeking to fulfill within ourselves. It may end in a breakup, loss of friendship or religion, etc., but we're all searching, for that sense of fulfillment, security and acceptance. And why that person's need led to a loss of something, it can add to the building up of another. We get lost in others sometimes because of the negative experiences we endure. In our minds we take those experiences and choose which parts we want to hold on to and let go. Most of the time the experiences we hold on to are those that we use as mental blocks to prevent a potential reoccurrence of a familiar situation. It is an irrational way of thinking, and here are some reasons why:

1. It will lead you away from the exploration of the truth. The mental block will create disillusionment of the role you or others may have played in your previous situation. Meaning, some persons are ALL BAD and you and other persons are ALL GOOD. This mental block can create blinders that prevent you from seeing the truth in others that will cause discomfort. It may also cause discomfort with you addressing your own truth.

2. Stunts maturation. I'm a firm believer that every experience is a learning lesson. Once you learn the lesson you are able to take those tools to attack new situations.

That can't happen when you disallow yourself to mature emotionally.

3. Every situation is not what you went through before. If so, it's time that you revisit the previous chapter and start doing some true self-assessment.

P.S. You don't have to beg people to be a part of your life! You're enough!

Hazardous Thoughts vs. BOLD Thoughts

List some of your **Hazardous thoughts**. Thoughts that hold you back, ruin relationships, friendships and other. Thoughts that you have a mental tug a war with. Thoughts that you don't want to have, but you struggle with letting them go. Then write a **BOLD thought to** interrupt that hazardous thought. It is good practice to use stop thought exercises to prevent the hazardous and irrational thoughts from taking over our lives.

Hazardous Thoughts   **BOLD Thoughts**

_____   _____
_____   _____
_____   _____
_____   _____
_____   _____
_____   _____
_____   _____
_____   _____
_____   _____
_____   _____
_____   _____
_____   _____
_____   _____
_____   _____
_____   _____
_____   _____

Friendships

There is no way I could complete this project without addressing a huge part of our very beings—friends. Friends have always been a major part of my life. In fact, I have the same friends since elementary school and picked up a few more along the way. You need friends to get in trouble with you, to love you, admonish you, to cry with you, laugh with you, and experience life with you. I've often heard women say they don't get along with other women, and I never understood that "philosophy." The times I have spent with my friends have been beautiful and an example of God's grace over my life.

Friendships can be tricky. I heard a preacher once say, "Some people suck up so much energy being hateful that when they leave a room, it lights up." Many times, we're stuck with what to do with those types of friends, or we're holding on to friendships void of support, care, sacrifice, or presence and that can be a source of self-inflicted pain. Years do not equate friendship; it's other little special things that do. It's the things you offer gratitude to God for because you know He is the Creator of all things good, the love, sacrifice, uncontrollable laughter, support in good and bad times, it's knowing that person is "solid" no matter the situation. Be comfortable with removing situations and people from your life that aren't adding to your well-being. It is hard, but trust me, when you no longer have that person around that you have allowed to make you feel low and bullied or not good enough, life will feel less like you're in a pressure cooker.

What kind of friend are you? Can you answer *yes* and provide examples? If *no*, jot down your answers *why not* in order to begin taking a look at your flow pattern (CBT flow model) to understand what you can do to change your outcomes.

Dependable _____

Loyal _____

Trusting _____

Caring _____

Shows up _____

Considerate _____

Supportive _____

Peaceable _____

Prayerful _____

Friendships, like romantic relationships, is an area that we respond to based off of experiences. We will mask being mean as being caring, instead of admitting the challenge with our vulnerability or perhaps some unresolved part of our CBT flow model we haven't addressed. Let's be clear; *it is unnecessary to be mean* for any reason. Think about it; when people get married, they love each other. What if they yelled their vows at each other and then ended with *I love you*? Seems unfitting. If you care about someone, then do that. If you believe in someone, then do that. Incongruency is not only an emotional and psychological pattern; unaddressed, it can become the dagger that slaughters any attachment that an individual may attempt to form.

If you struggle with making friends, start doing the work by determining the reasons for that pattern. P.S. You don't have to beg people to be a part of your life! You're enough! But it's healthy practice to evaluate ourselves.

What are qualities of a good friend? The next few entries are anonymous testimonies from various women of different ages and different walks of life, answering the question: What does being a friend mean to you? *or* What do you need from a friend?

"It's the foundation on which I try to build all relationships. It's a sisterhood of women who can depend on each other. A relationship of honesty, trust, and mutual respect. It's sometimes the family or siblings you never had, but always wanted. It's a special relationship that can happen at the drop of a hat or after life experience together."

—Anonymous, age 34.

"At age thirty-four, and now that I'm older, friendship is no longer about who's good company socially and who has the juiciest gossip. Now it's about matching energies and honoring each other as whole individuals—the good and bad parts of us. Friendship is constant support through adversity. Not only do friends celebrate each other and their wins, but they also provide a safe space where truths can be told and the love is not affected."
—*Anonymous, age 34*

"As a woman, I've had many friendships since my childhood years. I'm still friends with some, and then there are those that I have dissolved or have lost ties. Those I've remained friends with have similar character/personality, interests, hobbies, etc. I have learned that I'm most comfortable with friends that have or share similar qualities. I have friends or acquaintances who may have qualities that differ, but I'm not as close to them. As I've aged, I've learned more about myself, my personality and how this relates to those in my circle."
—*Anonymous, age 44*

"Friendship is a very important part of life. My perspective has shifted about this topic over the years. I've always loved having friends, this one constant. During my younger years, it seemed easy to make friends, no kid was a stranger, just a friend I hadn't met yet. I sometimes was swayed to do things for fear of judgement of friends. Sometimes, I would even disregard some better, loyal friends to get newer popular friends, not proud of that. Overall, friendship was easy. During my teenage years, I experienced an untimely death of a dear friend at fifteen and my closer friends became much more important. Many very good friends helped me get through tough times. Friendship got a little harder, more responsibilities, everyone more spread out, but still felt satisfied and friendship was still in abundance. In my adult years, friendship is *so* important, but *so* hard to maintain and start fresh. I miss my friends. I am blessed to have made great friends in my youth that I still connect with, because if it weren't for them, I would have three friends, one of them being my husband. While I am becoming more involved in women's groups and finding more fulfillment from that, it is still very hard. Things are more complicated as adults, but friendship is still important"

—*Anonymous, age 34*

"Now in our thirties, we've developed emotionally, mentally, even spiritually. Our friendships are based on deeper connections and having conversations about things that have meaning or a desire in our lives. I appreciate these connections. I also feel that our commonality has strengthened as I am more in tune with my faith and wanting to listen to and learn from people about life's issues. I am happier sitting at dinner or coffee talking with a friend than I am doing something else."

—*Anonymous, age 40*

" What I need from a friend is an emotional support system, someone who helps boost my self-confidence, a person who is willing to go through everything together and for them to be a loving caring individual."

—*Anonymous, age 16*

"Honesty. Sincerity. Trust. A true friend has all threee of these. They are honest to you, even when what they are saying is not what you want to hear or hurts. You know that what they are saying comes from a place of love. You can trust them to be sincere in their actions because they want the best for you. They have your back and are there to support you and pick you up or give you a lock on the pants when it's needed. The trust is integral to being able to feel safe to show your true self. To know that it's okay for you to have flaws because they are not judging you for them. They love you with all of the flaws, but that doesn't mean they won't call you on your crap."

—*Anonymous, age 50*

"I have never trusted or gotten close to anyone for fear of people not liking me. I had an outgoing boyfriend who loved to be around people and because of him, I now have several amazing friends."

—*Anonymous, age 24*

"As an individual, I've grown so much, more so in the last year. I've learned so much about myself and how I behave in almost all situations: interpersonal conflict, time management, mobility issues, unfamiliar/uncomfortable environments. While most of these instances didn't make me feel great at the time, looking back, I can see how much I've gained from the experience. I decided what I did and didn't like based on how some situations made me feel. I learned responsibility for my own actions, and how to deal with other people and their emotions."

—*Anonymous, age 19*

"With so many changes in my life, it seemed like trying to please everyone never brought me happiness, so in the last few months, I have made a lot of changes that would benefit me. I set goals for myself and accurately kept track of them (or found friends, family, or professors that would help keep me accountable). I think all the adversity I've faced in the last year has shaped me into the person I am today. I'm choosing to keep balance in my life by making sure I am on top of my schoolwork, remembering to stay connected with the people that matter the most, and taking time for myself every day so I can go through life without regrets."

—*Anonymous, age unknown*

Basically, we want to be accepted and genuinely connected to other individuals. We want that *Friends, Living Single*, or *Saved by the Bell* type of friendship. If you were that timid child no one wanted to play with, or the awkward kid that felt like you never fit in, or the kid that had it all, but never felt like you had genuine relationships, or the bigger kid, darker kid, lighter kid, proper kid; no matter what your experiences were, you are capable of having healthy relationships that are out there waiting for you to open your arms and embrace them.

I Smile
By Terri M. Bolds

I smile because I'm free

Traveling down long dark roads never turning toward the light

Because I didn't want to see the me, that I always thought I'd be

Hurt, rejected, unfamiliar and unimportant

But you set me free

Thank you me, because we traveled some rough times and I never thought I would be free

But me, you set me free

To laugh at the silly things I do, and to
embrace the love my mind kept from me

Me, I thank you for finally releasing the Me
that I have grown to be

The me, that is finally free

Let It Go

GUILT

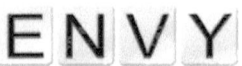

Bold Self-Reflection: Know Thyself | 39

As women, we carry the weight of the world on our shoulders. A popular song by Erykah Badu titled "Bag Lady" talks about how carrying so much baggage boggles you down, causing you to miss opportunities because you're lugging so much stuff—pain, anger, grief, embarrassment, envy, abandonment, etc. Let me be the first to offer you a hug through the pages of this book. A hug to let you know it is okay to feel and release. A hug to let you know the mistakes you made are forgiven. A hug to let you know you can manage your addictions. A hug to let you know the partner you chose that ruined your life will have to deal with God. A hug to let you know the parent that abused you was scarred, too, and you were not deserving of it. A hug to let you know your life matters. Life is great, but life is hard. Many times we are the reason our lives are hard because we stay mentally enslaved to our traumatic pasts, mistakes, and challenges. Believing there is something better seems impossible when all you know is hell.

Let *It* Go. Not only do you need to let it go, because there is nothing you can do to reverse the past, but baggage can literally kill you. An article titled "Best To Not Sweat The Small Stuff Because it Can Kill You," (NPR, 2014), discusses how chronic stress can kill you and how elevated levels of what is referred to as the "stress" hormone, cortisol, can interfere with learning and memory, lower your immune functioning and bone density, and increase the blood pressure and your chances of having high cholesterol and heart disease.

Let's pause for a brief moment and address the following questions:

What things are you holding on to? _____
_____
_____

How are they impacting your life? _____
_____
_____

What is the reality about those situations? _____
_____
_____

I sent a message to someone struggling with an estranged relationship with their father:

"We can't put expectations on people that they are unwilling or unable to fulfill. We have an innate feeling to want our parents. Some are just unequipped to fulfill those roles because of their own life experiences. It doesn't stop the hurt. But once we are able accept that each one of us comes with our own "stuff" we then have a responsibility to act accordingly. Unfortunately, you may never get what you're longing for. I had some father figures, but they weren't mine. They were other peoples. I wasn't their priority or apple of their eyes."

My male role models were great to me beyond what I could have imagined, but I still was not their daughter and that feeling has always been lingering.

From the moment of my father's cancer diagnosis, I was able to spend a few weeks with him before he passed. I'm grateful for that time we shared. I was visiting him in the hospital the day after he was given his prognosis and life expectancy. We talked about a lot—his health and other random things.

He spoke with my mom on the phone, and as I was putting my coat on to leave, he said, "I'm sorry for our relationship and as long as I am still living, we can make it right." Then, he told me to give him a hug. I didn't want to let go. I was so overcome with emotion that if I had uttered one word, I would have cried profusely.

It was the feeling I had been waiting for my whole life. You know how when you know what you feel is real, but until it's confirmed you're just kind of haunted with the idea that maybe you are imagining the situation? That is how I felt about things with my father.

It's funny; it wasn't until my father became ill that I saw his feet for the first time and realized I inherited his big toe. That may seem weird, but these were things I hadn't known about him. To my surprise, he also dyed his hair and we laughed about that because I didn't know that either. I learned more about my father during his dying days than I had known my whole life.

Now, go back to the moment he hugged me, I've always said that at any time I could make amends, it would be a new day for me. I have always wanted my father. When I was a kid, he was a tall, dark, handsome, smell-good wonder. I used to stand in the window whenever he was picking me up, which was one to two times a year, and wait for whatever big named car he was driving at the time to pull to the side of the house. Then, my stomach would be in knots; it would be like I was going with a stranger each time because it was hard to connect when you rarely saw or talked to someone.

That day in the hospital, I acknowledged him talking by saying, "Mmmhmm," because if I had uttered one word, I would have broken down and, perhaps, into uncontrollable tears.

Each time I saw my father, he hugged me. I've always been awkward with hugs and I'm a very unaffectionate person, so it is very rare that I will initiate a hug. But that day! That day, as my ill father lay in the bed, after having apologized for dozing off or for not being able to get up, told me to give him a hug; it was something I have never felt. When I leaned down and hugged him, I didn't want to let him go. I wanted that moment to last forever. At that moment, for the first time, I wanted to say, "Daddy, don't go," but I was experiencing some kind of paralysis. For those quick moments, nothing else mattered but my father's embrace. I even imagined laying with him, if only the bed were big enough.

Over the next few weeks, my father and I enjoyed each other's company. I arrived at the hospital the day he passed before anyone else. He was complaining to the nurses about them disturbing him and I walked in, asking what was going on. I asked him if it was okay if I sat with him for a while, and the last words I heard my father say to me were, "Yeah, yeah, you're my daughter."

Many will discredit my feelings regarding my father's death, and I have to live with the understanding that it's their right to feel how they feel, but it is my right to own the peace with which my father and I created in the last days we spent together. Have you ever been so hurt that your feelings cry? I never knew it was possible until now.

Use your experience as a testimony rather than a hindrance or tool that sabotages you. We have to make hard choices and sometimes those choices aren't favorable and many may not understand, but you have to do what is beneficial for your well-being. I am a huge advocate of pampering your emotional and mental health.

I have come to understand that forgiving someone is not letting them off the hook for the offense they caused. Forgiveness is instructed by God, and a healing for you. Waking up angry every day, or deciding not to trust every day, or being bitter every day is exhausting. It takes a lot of energy to remember to be that way daily. Forgiveness frees up space for you to live a life according to the will of God. It allows His love to permeate through you in a way that you can acknowledge is there. When you're bitter and angry all the time, it's a tad hard to believe God has your back.

Self-reflection break:

What is something you need to forgive someone for? _____

_____
_____
_____
_____
_____
_____

What is something you need to forgive yourself for? _____

_____
_____
_____
_____
_____
_____

How has not forgiving impacted your life? _____

_____
_____
_____
_____
_____
_____

Self-You

This last section will be bullet points because they seem to capture the most important points of a lesson, so here we go:

- You can never be the truest form of yourself if you're in a constant state of reinventing your dreams, desires, and falsifying your wants to conform into someone else's space! Create your own space!

- We need restoration. There's an old church hymn, titled "Restore My Soul." Our hearts get weary, our cups get empty and we need more strength. Call on God or your Higher Power to help restore you from the pile of disarray that you now wallow in.

- Allow yourself to fill vacant spaces in the universe that are yearning for artistry, dignity, integrity and ingenuity. Understand that divinity created you and, therefore, you're lacking nothing but personal drive. The suitcase of blame is full of articles of you.

- All my life I've felt like I have been waiting for someone to have my back in an unconditional way—affirming me, praising me, bragging about me—when in reality, I needed to be the level of unconditional love that I sought from those around me. God created us to be together. There is a level of love and belonging that we need to flourish, but at some point WE, I, YOU have to take the torch to light our own flame.

- Be Assertive-Love yourself, stop people pleasing, be okay with your decisions. This is your life.

Learn types of judgment:

- Constructive: Intended to correct, guide, encourage, educate.

- Destructive: Intended to destroy, tear down, weaken and belittle.

Self-care is not only pedicures and manicures, it is nurturing your mental health, flourishing your love, and growing in wisdom.

Frankie Beverly said in his song that when you find who you are, that's the "Golden Time of Day." Don't let your "Golden Time of Day" be your last day.

Stop shaming God by responding that you're "okay." I heard a speaker say, "How dare we say we're just okay?" Do you know how precious life is, how the many parts of your body work together to wake you up? How science can even explain all the complexities of life? You're blessed in joyous times and sad times; it's up to you to flip that stinking thinking lense. Start living a life that will have you shouting, "I'm Grrrrrrreat."

Self-Fulfilling Prophecy means that whatever you believe to be true can come to pass. Stop believing your life to be meaningless and instead, live it as purposeful. So when you look at your self-reflection, what do you see…?

Gratitude

My self-reflection wasn't always one of gratitude, but now when I look at my reflection, I see much more. I see that my life's struggles had to happen to build my testimony. I see that my life has been good and many times I have let the bad overshadow the starry fairytale memories of my past.

I serve a most High God that whispered in people's ears to speak to me and they obeyed. I'm grateful for their obedience because without it, who knows where I would be.

I am grateful for my parents giving me life, my mom for stressing education, and my friends for loving me and supporting me. Especially those friends who traveled this journey with me.

I am grateful to family members who have dropped gems in my lap my whole life.

I am grateful to my educators that went above and beyond.

I am grateful to the church for showing me the love of God when the world blinded me.

In closing, choose you. I haven't always loved my self-reflection, but now that I'm looking at myself with a new set of eyes and mind, I love every bit of what I see. Choose to live the best life you can live, no matter the hand you were dealt and take charge of your life and live it genuinely and wonderfully.

www.ingramcontent.com/pod-product-compliance
Lightning Source LLC
Chambersburg PA
CBHW060344080526
44584CB00013B/911